Cultures

Julie Haydon

Cultures

Text: Julie Haydon
Editor: Rebecca Crisp
Design: Jess Kelly
Series design: James Lowe
Photo researcher: Corrina Tauschke
Production controller: Lisa Porter

Acknowledgements
The author and publisher would like to acknowledge permission to reproduce material from the following sources:
AAP Image/COMSTOCK: p. 10 (bottom); Alamy: pp. 6 (bottom), 7 (top), 12; Corbis: pp. 4, 7 (bottom); Getty Images: pp. 3, 5 (bottom), 9, 11 (bottom left), 14; Masterfile: pp. 6 (centre), 11 (top); Photolibrary: pp. 1, 5 (top), 6 (top), 8 (top and centre), 10 (top), 11 (bottom right), 13, 15, cover, back cover;
Shutterstock.com © Denise Kappa, 2008 used under licence from Shutterstock.com: p. 8 (bottom).

Fast Forward Independent Texts
Level 7

ISBN 978 0 17 017942 3
ISBN 978 0 17 017896 9 (set)

Cengage Learning Australia
Level 7, 80 Dorcas Street
South Melbourne, Victoria Australia 3205
Phone: 1300 790 853

Cengage Learning New Zealand
Unit 4B Rosedale Office Park
331 Rosedale Road, Albany, North Shore NZ 0632
Phone: 0800 449 725

For learning solutions, visit **cengage.com.au**

Printed in Australia by Ligare Pty Ltd
7 8 9 10 23 22 21

Cultures

Julie Haydon

Contents

CHAPTER 1

A Way of Life

A **culture** is the way of life of a group of people.

Some cultures are very different from other cultures.

There are lots of different cultures in the world.
Each country has a different culture, and some have many cultures.

a wedding in Australia

a wedding in Vietnam

People learn about their culture from their family and other people.

Most people in a culture think and act in the same ways.

Most people in a culture have the same customs. Customs are the ways people do things. Most customs have been around for a long time.

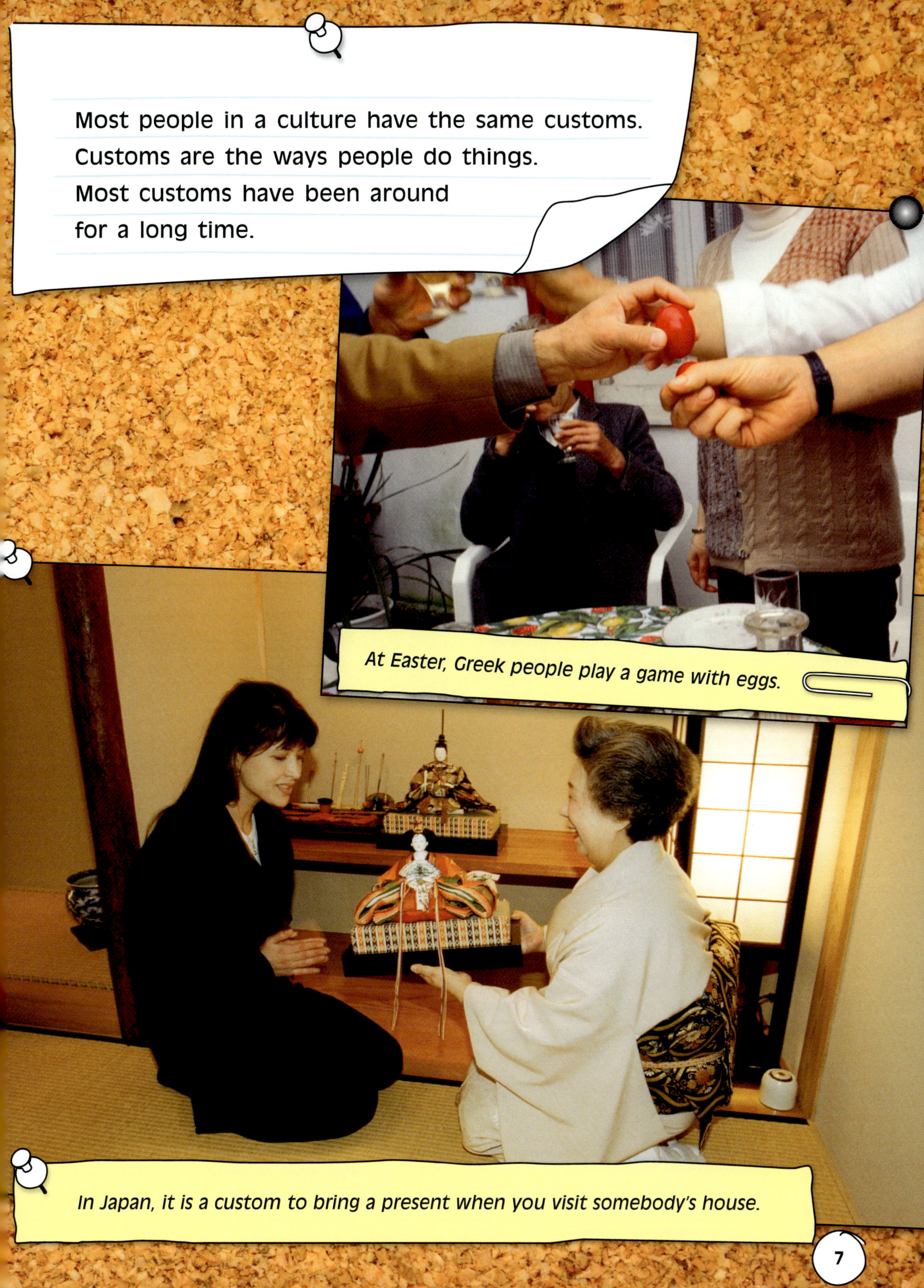

At Easter, Greek people play a game with eggs.

In Japan, it is a custom to bring a present when you visit somebody's house.

Most people in a culture

- dress and talk the same way
- cook and eat the same kinds of food
- live in the same kinds of homes

- play the same kinds of games
- **celebrate** in the same way.

These children are playing with a piñata full of lollies.

CHAPTER 2

Cultures Over Time

Cultures do not stay the same.
They change over time.

In many cultures, women used to do the cooking.

Now men and women often share the cooking.

Sometimes cultures change when people from different cultures meet.

Sometimes cultures change when people find new ways to do things.

Farmers used to cut crops with hand tools, but now crops are cut by a machine.

CHAPTER 3

Special Days

People can celebrate their culture on special days.

On these days, people eat special food and dress in special clothes.

Indian people celebrate a festival called Diwali every year.

People celebrate their culture's past. They also celebrate their culture as it is today.

Chinese New Year celebrations

CHAPTER 4

Different Cultures

Different cultures make other countries fun to go to.
It is good to learn about different cultures.

These people are visiting Morocco, in Africa.

There can be lots of different cultures in one country.
People move to different countries but they take their culture with them.

Glossary

celebrate to have a party for a special day or event

culture a way of living that includes food, clothes and manners

Index